AZ-900: MICROSOFT AZURE FUNDAMENTALS EXAM PRACTICE QUESTIONS & DUMPS WITH EXPLANATIONS

90+ EXAM PRACTICE QUESTIONS FOR AZ-900:
MICROSOFT AZURE FUNDAMENTALS EXAM
UPDATED 2020

Presented By: Vortex Books

VORTEX

Books

About Vortex Books:

Vortex Books is a publishing company based in San Francisco, California, USA, a platform that is available both online & locally, which unleashes the power of technical and educational content. Our aim is to provide help to individuals who are eager to learn and excel in technical certifications and other educational fields. Vortex Books was founded in 2017, and is now distributing books globally.

QUESTION 1

This question requires that you evaluate the underlined text to determine if it is correct.

When you are implementing a Software as a Service (SaaS) solution, you are responsible for <u>configuring high availability</u>.

Instructions: Review the underlined text. If it makes the statement correct, select "No change is needed". If the statement is incorrect, select the answer choice that makes the statement correct.

A. No change is needed.
B. defining scalability rules
C. installing the SaaS solution
D. configuring the SaaS solution

Correct Answer: D

Explanation/Reference:

Explanation:
When you are implementing a Software as a Service (SaaS) solution, you are responsible for configuring the SaaS solution. Everything else is managed by the cloud provider.

SaaS requires the least amount of management. The cloud provider is responsible for managing everything, and the end user just uses the software.

Software as a service (SaaS) allows users to connect to and use cloud-based apps over the Internet. Common examples are email, calendaring and office tools (such as Microsoft Office 365).

SaaS provides a complete software solution which you purchase on a pay-as-you-go basis from a cloud service provider. You rent the use of an app for your organization and your users connect to it over the Internet, usually with a web browser. All of the underlying infrastructure, middleware, app software and app data are located in the service provider's data center. The service provider manages the hardware and software and with the appropriate service agreement, will ensure the availability and the security of the app and your data as well.

References:

https://azure.microsoft.com/en-in/overview/what-is-saas/

https://docs.microsoft.com/en-gb/learn/modules/principles-cloud-computing/5-types-of-cloud-services

QUESTION 2

This question requires that you evaluate the underlined text to determine if it is correct.

An organization that hosts its infrastructure <u>in a private cloud</u> can close its data center.

Instructions: Review the underlined text. If it makes the statement correct, select "No change is needed". If the statement is incorrect, select the answer choice that makes the statement correct.

A. No change is needed.
B. in a hybrid cloud
C. in the public cloud
D. on a Hyper-V host

Correct Answer: C

Explanation/Reference:

Explanation:
A private cloud is hosted in your datacenter. Therefore, you cannot close your datacenter if you are using a private cloud. A public cloud is hosted externally, for example, in Microsoft Azure. An organization that hosts its infrastructure in a public cloud can close its data center.

Public cloud is the most common deployment model. In this case, you have no local hardware to manage or keep up-to-date – everything runs on your cloud provider's hardware. Microsoft Azure is an example of a public cloud provider.

In a private cloud, you create a cloud environment in your own datacenter and provide self-service access to compute resources to users in your organization. This offers a simulation of a public cloud to your users, but you remain completely responsible for the purchase and maintenance of the hardware and software services you provide.

References:
https://docs.microsoft.com/en-gb/learn/modules/principles-cloud-computing/4-cloud-deployment-models

QUESTION 3

What are two characteristics of the public cloud? Each correct answer presents a complete solution.

A. dedicated hardware
B. unsecured connections
C. limited storage
D. metered pricing
E. self-service management

Correct Answer: DE

Explanation/Reference:

Explanation:
With the public cloud, you get pay-as-you-go pricing – you pay only for what you use, no CapEx costs.
With the public cloud, you have self-service management. You are responsible for the deployment and configuration of the cloud resources such as virtual machines or web sites. The underlying hardware that hosts the cloud resources is managed by the cloud provider.

Incorrect Answers:
A: You don't have dedicated hardware. The underlying hardware is shared so you could have multiple customers using cloud resources hosted on the same physical hardware.
B: Connections to the public cloud are secure.
C: Storage is not limited. You can have as much storage as you like.

References:
https://docs.microsoft.com/en-gb/learn/modules/principles-cloud-computing/4-cloud-deployment-models

QUESTION 4

Note: This question is part of a series of questions that present the same scenario. Each question in the series contains a unique solution that might meet the stated goals. Some question sets might have more than one correct solution, while others might not have a correct solution.

Your company plans to migrate all its data and resources to Azure.

The company's migration plan states that only Platform as a Service (PaaS) solutions must be used in Azure. You need to deploy an Azure environment that meets the company migration plan.

Solution: You create an Azure App Service and Azure SQL databases.

Does this meet the goal?

A. Yes
B. No

Correct Answer: A

Explanation/Reference:

Explanation:
Azure App Service and Azure SQL databases are examples of Azure PaaS solutions. Therefore, this solution does meet the goal.

QUESTION 5

Note: This question is part of a series of questions that present the same scenario. Each question in the series contains a unique solution that might meet the stated goals. Some question sets might have more than one correct solution, while others might not have a correct solution.

Your company plans to migrate all its data and resources to Azure.

The company's migration plan states that only Platform as a Service (PaaS) solutions must be used in Azure. You need to deploy an Azure environment that meets the company migration plan.

Solution: You create an Azure App Service and Azure Storage accounts. Does this meet the goal?

A. Yes
B. No

Correct Answer: B

Explanation/Reference:

Explanation:
Azure App Service is a PaaS (Platform as a Service) service. However, Azure Storage accounts are an IaaS (Infrastructure as a Service) service. Therefore, this solution does not meet the goal.

QUESTION 6

Your company hosts an accounting application named App1 that is used by all the customers of the company.

App1 has low usage during the first three weeks of each month and very high usage during the last week of each month. Which benefit of Azure Cloud Services supports cost management for this type of usage pattern?

A. high availability
B. high latency
C. elasticity
D. load balancing

Correct Answer: C

Explanation/Reference:

Explanation:
Elasticity in this case is the ability to provide additional compute resource when needed and reduce the compute resource when not needed to reduce costs. Autoscaling is an example of elasticity.

Elastic computing is the ability to quickly expand or decrease computer processing, memory and storage resources to meet changing demands without worrying about capacity planning and engineering for peak usage. Typically controlled by system monitoring tools, elastic computing matches the amount of resources allocated to the amount of resources actually needed without disrupting operations. With cloud elasticity, a company avoids paying for unused capacity or idle resources and doesn't have to worry about investing in the purchase or maintenance of additional resources and equipment.

References:
https://azure.microsoft.com/en-gb/overview/what-is-elastic-computing/

QUESTION 7

You plan to migrate a web application to Azure. The web application is accessed by external users.

You need to recommend a cloud deployment solution to minimize the amount of administrative effort used to manage the web application. What should you include in the recommendation?

A. Software as a Service (SaaS)
B. Platform as a Service (PaaS)
C. Infrastructure as a Service (IaaS)
D. Database as a Service (DaaS)

Correct Answer: B

Explanation/Reference:

Explanation:
Azure App Service is a platform-as-a-service (PaaS) offering that lets you create web and mobile apps for any platform or device and connect to data anywhere, in the cloud or on-premises. App Service includes the web and mobile capabilities that were previously delivered separately as Azure Websites and Azure Mobile Services.

References:
https://docs.microsoft.com/en-us/azure/security/fundamentals/paas-applications-using-app-services

QUESTION 8

You have an on-premises network that contains 100 servers.

You need to recommend a solution that provides additional resources to your users. The solution must minimize capital and operational expenditure costs. What should you include in the recommendation?

A. a complete migration to the public cloud
B. an additional data center
C. a private cloud
D. a hybrid cloud

Correct Answer: D

Explanation/Reference:

Explanation:
A hybrid cloud is a combination of a private cloud and a public cloud.
Capital expenditure is the spending of money up-front for infrastructure such as new servers.

With a hybrid cloud, you can continue to use the on-premises servers while adding new servers in the public cloud (Azure for example). Adding new servers in Azure minimizes the capital expenditure costs as you are not paying for new servers as you would if you deployed new server on-premises.

Incorrect Answers:
A: A complete migration of 100 servers to the public cloud would involve a lot of operational expenditure (the cost of migrating all the servers).

B: An additional data center would involve a lot of capital expenditure (the cost of the new infrastructure).
C: A private cloud is hosted on on-premises servers to this would involve a lot of capital expenditure (the cost of the new infrastructure to host the private cloud).

References:
https://docs.microsoft.com/en-gb/learn/modules/principles-cloud-computing/4-cloud-deployment-models

QUESTION 9

Note: This question is part of a series of questions that present the same scenario. Each question in the series contains a unique solution that might meet the stated goals. Some question sets might have more than one correct solution, while others might not have a correct solution.

You plan to deploy several Azure virtual machines.

You need to ensure that the services running on the virtual machines are available if a single data center fails. Solution: You deploy the virtual machines to two or more scale sets. Does this meet the goal?

A. Yes
B. No

Correct Answer: B

Explanation/Reference:

Explanation:
This answer does not specify that the scale set will be configured across multiple data centers so this solution does not meet the goal.

Azure virtual machine scale sets let you create and manage a group of load balanced VMs. The number of VM instances can automatically increase or decrease in response to demand or a defined schedule. Scale sets provide high availability to your applications, and allow you to centrally manage, configure, and update many VMs.

Virtual machines in a scale set can be deployed across multiple update domains and fault domains to maximize availability and resilience to outages due to data center outages, and planned or unplanned maintenance events.

Reference:
https://docs.microsoft.com/en-us/azure/virtual-machine-scale-sets/availability

QUESTION 10

Note: This question is part of a series of questions that present the same scenario. Each question in the series contains a unique solution that might meet the stated goals. Some question sets might have more than one correct solution, while others might not have a correct solution.

You plan to deploy several Azure virtual machines.

You need to ensure that the services running on the virtual machines are available if a single data center fails. Solution: You deploy the virtual machines to two or more availability zones.
Does this meet the goal?

A. Yes
B. No

Correct Answer: A

Explanation/Reference:

Explanation:
Availability zones expand the level of control you have to maintain the availability of the applications and data on your VMs. An Availability Zone is a physically separate zone, within an Azure region. There are three Availability Zones per supported Azure region.

Each Availability Zone has a distinct power source, network, and cooling. By architecting your solutions to use replicated VMs in zones, you can protect your apps and data from the loss of a datacenter. If one zone is compromised, then replicated apps and data are instantly available in another zone.

Reference:
https://docs.microsoft.com/en-us/azure/virtual-machine-scale-sets/availability

QUESTION 11

Note: This question is part of a series of questions that present the same scenario. Each question in the series contains a unique solution that might meet the stated goals. Some question sets might have more than one correct solution, while others might not have a correct solution.

You plan to deploy several Azure virtual machines.

You need to ensure that the services running on the virtual machines are available if a single data center fails.

Solution: You deploy the virtual machines to two or more regions. Does this meet the goal?

A. Yes
B. No

Correct Answer: A

Explanation/Reference:

Explanation:
By deploying the virtual machines to two or more regions, you are deploying the virtual machines to multiple datacenters. This will ensure that the services running on the virtual machines are available if a single data center fails.

Azure operates in multiple datacenters around the world. These datacenters are grouped in to geographic regions, giving you flexibility in choosing where to build your applications.

You create Azure resources in defined geographic regions like 'West US', 'North Europe', or 'Southeast Asia'. You can review the list of regions and their locations. Within each region, multiple datacenters exist to provide for redundancy and availability.

Reference:
https://docs.microsoft.com/en-us/azure/virtual-machines/windows/regions

QUESTION 12

You have 1,000 virtual machines hosted on the Hyper-V hosts in a data center.

You plan to migrate all the virtual machines to an Azure pay-as-you-go subscription. You need to identify which expenditure model to use for the planned Azure solution. Which expenditure model should you identify?

A. operational
B. elastic
C. capital
D. scalable

Correct Answer: A

Explanation/Reference:

Explanation:
One of the major changes that you will face when you move from on-premises cloud to the public cloud is the switch from capital expenditure (buying hardware) to operating expenditure (paying for service as you use it). This switch also requires more careful management of your costs. The benefit of the cloud is that you can fundamentally and positively affect the cost of a service you use by merely shutting down or resizing it when it's not needed.

References:
https://docs.microsoft.com/en-us/azure/architecture/cloud-adoption/appendix/azure-scaffold

QUESTION 13

You plan to provision Infrastructure as a Service (IaaS) resources in Azure. Which resource is an example of IaaS?

A. an Azure web app
B. an Azure virtual machine
C. an Azure logic app
D. an Azure SQL database

Correct Answer: B

Explanation/Reference:

Explanation:
An Azure virtual machine is an example of Infrastructure as a Service (IaaS).

Azure web app, Azure logic app and Azure SQL database are all examples of Platform as a Service (Paas).

References:
https://azure.microsoft.com/en-gb/overview/what-is-iaas/

https://azure.microsoft.com/en-gb/overview/what-is-paas/

QUESTION 14

A team of developers at your company plans to deploy, and then remove, 50 virtual machines each week. All the virtual machines are configured by using Azure Resource Manager templates.

You need to recommend which Azure service will minimize the administrative effort required to deploy and remove the virtual machines. What should you recommend?

A. Azure Reserved Virtual Machine (VM) Instances
B. Azure DevTest Labs
C. Azure virtual machine scale sets
D. Microsoft Managed Desktop

Correct Answer: B

Explanation/Reference:

Explanation:
DevTest Labs creates labs consisting of pre-configured bases or Azure Resource Manager templates. By using DevTest Labs, you can test the latest versions of your applications by doing the following tasks:

- Quickly provision Windows and Linux environments by using reusable templates and artifacts.
- Easily integrate your deployment pipeline with DevTest Labs to provision on-demand environments.
- Scale up your load testing by provisioning multiple test agents and create pre-provisioned environments for training and demos.

Reference:
https://docs.microsoft.com/en-us/azure/lab-services/devtest-lab-overview

QUESTION 15

Note: This question is part of a series of questions that present the same scenario. Each question in the series contains a unique solution that might meet the stated goals. Some question sets might have more than one correct solution, while others might not have a correct solution.

You plan to deploy several Azure virtual machines.

You need to ensure that the services running on the virtual machines are available if a single data center fails. Solution: You deploy the virtual machines to two or more resource groups.
Does this meet the goal?

A. Yes

B. No

Correct Answer: B

Explanation/Reference:

Explanation:
A resource group is a logical container for Azure resources. When you create a resource group, you specify which location to create the resource group in. However, when you create a virtual machine and place it in the resource group, the virtual machine can still be in a different location (different datacenter). Therefore, creating multiple resource groups, even if they are in separate datacenters does not ensure that the services running on the virtual machines are available if a single data center fails.

References:
https://docs.microsoft.com/en-us/azure/azure-resource-manager/management/overview#resource-groups

QUESTION 16

Note: This question is part of a series of questions that present the same scenario. Each question in the series contains a unique solution that might meet the stated goals. Some question sets might have more than one correct solution, while others might not have a correct solution.

Your company plans to migrate all its data and resources to Azure.

The company's migration plan states that only Platform as a Service (PaaS) solutions must be used in Azure. You need to deploy an Azure environment that meets the company migration plan.
Solution: You create an Azure virtual machines, Azure SQL databases, and Azure Storage accounts. Does this meet the goal?

A. Yes
B. No

Correct Answer: A

Explanation/Reference:

Explanation:

Platform as a service (PaaS) is a complete development and deployment environment in the cloud. PaaS includes infrastructure—servers, storage, and networking —but also middleware, development tools, business intelligence (BI) services, database management systems, and more. PaaS is designed to support the complete web application lifecycle: building, testing, deploying, managing, and updating.

References:
https://azure.microsoft.com/en-us/overview/what-is-paas/

QUESTION 17

Your company plans to deploy several custom applications to Azure. The applications will provide invoicing services to the customers of the company. Each application will have several prerequisite applications and services installed.

You need to recommend a cloud deployment solution for all the applications. What should you recommend?

A. Software as a Service (SaaS)

B. Platform as a Service (PaaS)

C. Infrastructure as a Service (IaaS)

Correct Answer: C

Explanation/Reference:
Explanation:
Infrastructure as a service (IaaS) is an instant computing infrastructure, provisioned and managed over the internet. The IaaS service provider manages the infrastructure, while you purchase, install, configure, and manage your own software

Incorrect Answers:
A: Software as a service (SaaS) allows users to connect to and use cloud-based apps over the Internet. Common examples are email, calendaring, and office tools. In this scenario, you need to run your own apps, and therefore require an infrastructure.

B:
Platform as a service (PaaS) is a complete development and deployment environment in the cloud. PaaS includes infrastructure—servers, storage, and networking —but also middleware, development tools, business intelligence (BI) services, database management systems, and more. PaaS is designed to support the complete web application lifecycle: building, testing, deploying, managing, and updating.

References:
https://azure.microsoft.com/en-us/overview/what-is-iaas/
https://azure.microsoft.com/en-us/overview/what-is-saas/
https://azure.microsoft.com/en-us/overview/what-is-paas/

QUESTION 18

This question requires that you evaluate the underlined text to determine if it is correct.

An Azure region <u>contains one or more data centers that are connected by using a low-latency network</u>.

Instructions: Review the underlined text. If it makes the statement correct, select "No change is needed". If the statement is incorrect, select the answer choice that makes the statement correct.

A. No change is needed
B. Is found in each country where Microsoft has a subsidiary office
C. Can be found in every country in Europe and the Americas only
D. Contains one or more data centers that are connected by using a high-latency network

Correct Answer: A

Explanation/Reference:

Explanation:
A region is a set of data centres deployed within a latency-defined perimeter and connected through a dedicated regional low-latency network. Microsoft Azure currently has 55 regions worldwide.
Regions are divided into Availability Zones. Availability Zones are physically separate locations within an Azure region. Each Availability Zone is made up of one or more datacenters equipped with independent power, cooling, and networking.

References:
https://azure.microsoft.com/en-gb/global-infrastructure/regions/

QUESTION 19

This question requires that you evaluate the underlined text to determine if it is correct.

You plan to deploy 20 virtual machines to an Azure environment. To ensure that a virtual machine named VM1 cannot connect to the other virtual machines, VM1 must <u>be deployed to a separate virtual network</u>.

Instructions: Review the underlined text. If it makes the statement correct, select "No change is needed". If the statement is incorrect, select the answer choice that makes the statement correct.

A. No change is needed
B. run a different operating system than the other virtual machines
C. be deployed to a separate resource group
D. have two network interfaces

Correct Answer: A

Explanation/Reference:

Explanation:
Azure automatically routes traffic between subnets in a virtual network. Therefore, all virtual machines in a virtual network can connect to the other virtual machines in the same virtual network. Even if the virtual machines are on separate subnets within the virtual network, they can still communicate with each other.

To ensure that a virtual machine cannot connect to the other virtual machines, the virtual machine must be deployed to a separate virtual network.

References:
https://docs.microsoft.com/en-us/azure/virtual-network/virtual-networks-udr-overview

QUESTION 20

This question requires that you evaluate the underlined text to determine if it is correct.

When you need to delegate permissions to several Azure virtual machines simultaneously, you must deploy the Azure virtual machines <u>to the same Azure region</u>.

Instructions: Review the underlined text. If it makes the statement correct, select "No change is needed". If the statement is incorrect, select the answer choice that makes the statement correct.

A. No change is needed
B. by using the same Azure Resource Manager template
C. to the same resource group
D. to the same availability zone

Correct Answer: C

Explanation/Reference:

Explanation:
A resource group is a logical container for Azure resources. Resource groups make the management of Azure resources easier.

With a resource group, you can allow a user to manage all resources in the resource group, such as virtual machines, websites, and subnets. The permissions you apply to the resource group apply to all resources contained in the resource group.

References:
https://docs.microsoft.com/en-us/azure/azure-resource-manager/management/overview#resource-groups
https://docs.microsoft.com/en-us/azure/role-based-access-control/overview

QUESTION 21

A team of developers at your company plans to deploy, and then remove, 50 customized virtual machines each week. Thirty of the virtual machines run Windows Server 2016 and 20 of the virtual machines run Ubuntu Linux.

You need to recommend which Azure service will minimize the administrative effort required to deploy and remove the virtual machines.

What should you recommend?

A. Azure Reserved Virtual Machines (VM) Instances
B. Azure virtual machine scale sets
C. Azure DevTest Labs
D. Microsoft Managed Desktop

Correct Answer: C

Explanation/Reference:

Explanation:
DevTest Labs creates labs consisting of pre-configured bases or Azure Resource Manager templates. By using DevTest Labs, you can test the latest versions of your applications by doing the following tasks:
- Quickly provision Windows and Linux environments by using reusable templates and artifacts.
- Easily integrate your deployment pipeline with DevTest Labs to provision on-demand environments.
- Scale up your load testing by provisioning multiple test agents and create pre-provisioned environments for training and demos.

Reference:
https://docs.microsoft.com/en-us/azure/lab-services/devtest-lab-overview

QUESTION 22

This question requires that you evaluate the underlined text to determine if it is correct.

One of the benefits of Azure SQL Data Warehouse is that <u>high availability</u> is built into the platform.

Instructions: Review the underlined text. If it makes the statement correct, select "No change is needed". If the statement is incorrect, select the answer choice that makes the statement correct.

A. No change is needed
B. automatic scaling
C. data compression
D. versioning

Correct Answer: A

Explanation/Reference:

Explanation:
Azure Data Warehouse (now known as Azure Synapse Analytics) is a PaaS offering from Microsoft. As with all PaaS services from Microsoft, SQL Data Warehouse offers an availability SLA of 99.9%. Microsoft can offer 99.9% availability because it has high availability features built into the platform.

References:
https://docs.microsoft.com/en-us/azure/sql-data-warehouse/sql-data-warehouse-overview-faq

QUESTION 23

You plan to store 20 TB of data in Azure. The data will be accessed infrequently and visualized by using Microsoft Power BI. You need to recommend a storage solution for the data. Which two solutions should you recommend? Each correct answer presents a complete solution.

A. Azure Data Lake
B. Azure Cosmos DB
C. Azure SQL Data Warehouse
D. Azure SQL Database
E. Azure Database for PostgreSQL

Correct Answer: AC

Explanation/Reference:

Explanation:
You can use Power BI to analyze and visualize data stored in Azure Data Lake and Azure SQL Data Warehouse.

Azure Data Lake includes all of the capabilities required to make it easy for developers, data scientists and analysts to store data of any size and shape and at any speed, and do all types of processing and analytics across platforms and languages. It removes the complexities of ingesting and storing all your data while making it faster to get up and running with batch, streaming and interactive analytics. It also integrates seamlessly with operational stores and data warehouses so that you can extend current data applications.

References:
https://docs.microsoft.com/en-us/azure/data-lake-store/data-lake-store-power-bi https://azure.microsoft.com/en-gb/solutions/data-lake/ https://docs.microsoft.com/en-us/azure/data-lake-store/data-lake-store-power-bi

QUESTION 24

You need to identify the type of failure for which an Azure availability zone can be used to protect access to Azure services. What should you identify?

A. a physical server failure
B. an Azure region failure
C. a storage failure
D. an Azure data center failure

Correct Answer: D

Explanation/Reference:

Explanation:
Availability zones expand the level of control you have to maintain the availability of the applications and data on your VMs. An Availability Zone is a physically separate zone, within an Azure region. There are three Availability Zones per supported Azure region.

Each Availability Zone has a distinct power source, network, and cooling. By architecting your solutions to use replicated VMs in zones, you can protect your apps and data from the loss of a datacenter. If one zone is compromised, then replicated apps and data are instantly available in another zone.

Reference:
https://docs.microsoft.com/en-us/azure/virtual-machine-scale-sets/availability

QUESTION 25

You have a virtual machine named VM1 that runs Windows Server 2016. VM1 is in the East US Azure region.

Which Azure service should you use from the Azure portal to view service failure notifications that can affect the availability of VM1?

A. Azure Service Fabric
B. Azure Monitor
C. Azure virtual machines
D. Azure Advisor

Correct Answer: C

Explanation/Reference:

Explanation:
In the Azure virtual machines page in the Azure portal, there is a named Maintenance Status. This column will display service issues that could affect your virtual machine. A service failure is rare but host server maintenance that could affect your virtual machines is more common.

Azure periodically updates its platform to improve the reliability, performance, and security of the host infrastructure for virtual machines. The purpose of these updates ranges from patching software components in the hosting environment to upgrading networking components or decommissioning hardware.

References:
https://docs.microsoft.com/en-us/azure/virtual-machines/maintenance-and-updates

QUESTION 26

Note: This question is part of a series of questions that present the same scenario. Each question in the series contains a unique solution that might meet the stated goals. Some question sets might have more than one correct solution, while others might not have a correct solution.

An Azure administrator plans to run a PowerShell script that creates Azure resources. You need to recommend which computer configuration to use to run the script.

Solution: Run the script from a computer that runs Chrome OS and uses Azure Cloud Shell.

Does this meet the goal?

A. Yes
B. No

Correct Answer: A

Explanation/Reference:

Explanation:
A PowerShell script is a file that contains PowerShell cmdlets and code. A PowerShell script needs to be run in PowerShell.

With the Azure Cloud Shell, you can run PowerShell cmdlets and scripts in a Web browser. You log in to the Azure Portal and select the Azure Cloud Shell option. This will open a PowerShell session in the Web browser. The Azure Cloud Shell has the necessary Azure PowerShell module installed.

Note: to run a PowerShell script in the Azure Cloud Shell, you need to change to the directory where the PowerShell script is stored.

References:
https://docs.microsoft.com/en-us/azure/cloud-shell/quickstart-powershell

QUESTION 27

Note: This question is part of a series of questions that present the same scenario. Each question in the series contains a unique solution that might meet the stated goals. Some question sets might have more than one correct solution, while others might not have a correct solution.

An Azure administrator plans to run a PowerShell script that creates Azure resources. You need to recommend which computer configuration to use to run the script.

Solution: Run the script from a computer that runs macOS and has PowerShell Core 6.0 installed. Does this meet the goal?

A. Yes
B. No

Correct Answer: A

Explanation/Reference:

Explanation:
A PowerShell script is a file that contains PowerShell cmdlets and code. A PowerShell script needs to be run in PowerShell. In this question, the computer has PowerShell Core 6.0 installed. Therefore, this solution does meet the goal.

Note: To create Azure resources using PowerShell, you would need to import the Azure PowerShell module which includes the PowerShell cmdlets required to create the resources.

References:
https://docs.microsoft.com/en-us/powershell/scripting/components/ise/how-to-write-and-run-scripts-in-the-windows-powershell-ise?view=powershell-6

QUESTION 28

You have an Azure environment that contains 10 virtual networks and 100 virtual machines. You need to limit the amount of inbound traffic to all the Azure virtual networks. What should you create?

A. one application security group (ASG)
B. 10 virtual network gateways
C. 10 Azure ExpressRoute circuits
D. one Azure firewall

Correct Answer: D

Explanation/Reference:

Explanation:
You can restrict traffic to multiple virtual networks with a single Azure firewall.

Azure Firewall is a managed, cloud-based network security service that protects your Azure Virtual Network resources. It's a fully stateful firewall as a service with built-in high availability and unrestricted cloud scalability.

You can centrally create, enforce, and log application and network connectivity policies across subscriptions and virtual networks. Azure Firewall uses a static public IP address for your virtual network resources allowing outside firewalls to identify traffic originating from your virtual network.

References:
https://docs.microsoft.com/en-us/azure/firewall/overview

QUESTION 29

You have an Azure environment that contains multiple Azure virtual machines.

You plan to implement a solution that enables the client computers on your on-premises network to communicate to the Azure virtual machines. You need to recommend which Azure resources must be created for the planned solution.

Which two Azure resources should you include in the recommendation? Each correct answer presents part of the solution.

A. a virtual network gateway
B. a load balancer
C. an application gateway
D. a virtual network
E. a gateway subnet

Correct Answer: AE

Explanation/Reference:
Explanation:
To implement a solution that enables the client computers on your on-premises network to communicate to the Azure virtual machines, you need to configure a VPN (Virtual Private Network) to connect the on-premises network to the Azure virtual network.

The Azure VPN device is known as a Virtual Network Gateway. The virtual network gateway needs to be located in a dedicated subnet in the Azure virtual network. This dedicated subnet is known as a gateway subnet and must be named 'GatewaySubnet'.

Note: a virtual network (answer D) is also required. However, as we already have virtual machines deployed in a Azure, we can assume that the virtual network is already in place.

References:
https://docs.microsoft.com/en-us/office365/enterprise/connect-an-on-premises-network-to-a-microsoft-azure-virtual-network

QUESTION 30

Note: This question is part of a series of questions that present the same scenario. Each question in the series contains a unique solution that might meet the stated goals. Some question sets might have more than one correct solution, while others might not have a correct solution.

You have an Azure environment. You need to create a new Azure virtual machine from a tablet that runs the Android operating system. Solution: You use Bash in Azure Cloud Shell. Does this meet the goal?

A. Yes
B. No

Correct Answer: A

Explanation/Reference:

Explanation:
With Azure Cloud Shell, you can create virtual machines using Bash or PowerShell.

Azure Cloud Shell is an interactive, authenticated, browser-accessible shell for managing Azure resources. It provides the flexibility of choosing the shell experience that best suits the way you work, either Bash or PowerShell.

Reference:
https://docs.microsoft.com/en-us/azure/cloud-shell/quickstart
https://docs.microsoft.com/en-us/azure/cloud-shell/overview

QUESTION 31

Your company plans to move several servers to Azure.

The company's compliance policy states that a server named FinServer must be on a separate network segment. You are evaluating which Azure services can be used to meet the compliance policy requirements.
Which Azure solution should you recommend?

A. a resource group for FinServer and another resource group for all the other servers
B. a virtual network for FinServer and another virtual network for all the other servers
C. a VPN for FinServer and a virtual network gateway for each other server
D. one resource group for all the servers and a resource lock for FinServer

Correct Answer: B

Explanation/Reference:

Explanation:
Networks in Azure are known as virtual networks. A virtual network can have multiple IP address spaces and multiple subnets. Azure automatically routes traffic between different subnets within a virtual network.
The question states that FinServer must be on a separate network segment. The only way to separate FinServer from the other servers in networking terms is to place the server in a different virtual network to the other servers.

References:
https://docs.microsoft.com/en-us/azure/virtual-network/virtual-network-vnet-plan-design-arm

QUESTION 32

You plan to map a network drive from several computers that run Windows 10 to Azure Storage. You need to create a storage solution in Azure for the planned mapped drive.

What should you create?

A. an Azure SQL database
B. a virtual machine data disk
C. a Files service in a storage account
D. a Blobs service in a storage account

Correct Answer: C

Explanation/Reference:

Explanation:
Azure Files is Microsoft's easy-to-use cloud file system. Azure file shares can be seamlessly used in Windows and Windows Server.
To use an Azure file share with Windows, you must either mount it, which means assigning it a drive letter or mount point path, or access it via its UNC path.

Unlike other SMB shares you may have interacted with, such as those hosted on a Windows Server, Linux Samba server, or NAS device, Azure file shares do not currently support Kerberos authentication with your Active Directory (AD) or Azure Active Directory (AAD) identity, although this is a feature we are working on.
Instead, you must access your Azure file share with the storage account key for the storage account containing your Azure file share. A storage account key is an administrator key for a storage account, including administrator permissions to all files and folders within the file share you're accessing, and for all file shares and other storage resources (blobs, queues, tables, etc) contained within your storage account.

References:
https://docs.microsoft.com/en-us/azure/storage/files/storage-how-to-use-files-windows

QUESTION 33

Your company plans to migrate all its network resources to Azure. You need to start the planning process by exploring Azure.

What should you create first?

A. a subscription
B. a resource group
C. a virtual network
D. a management group

Correct Answer: A

Explanation/Reference:

Explanation:
The first thing you create in Azure is a subscription. You can think of an Azure subscription as an 'Azure account'. You get billed per subscription.

A subscription is an agreement with Microsoft to use one or more Microsoft cloud platforms or services, for which charges accrue based on either a per-user license fee or on cloud-based resource consumption.

Microsoft's Software as a Service (SaaS)-based cloud offerings (Office 365, Intune/EMS, and Dynamics 365) charge per-user license fees. Microsoft's Platform as a Service (PaaS) and Infrastructure as a Service (IaaS) cloud offerings (Azure) charge based on cloud resource consumption.

You can also use a trial subscription, but the subscription expires after a specific amount of time or consumption charges. You can convert a trial subscription to a paid subscription. Organizations can have multiple subscriptions for Microsoft's cloud offerings.

References:
https://docs.microsoft.com/en-us/office365/enterprise/subscriptions-licenses-accounts-and-tenants-for-microsoft-cloud-offerings

QUESTION 34

You have an on-premises application that sends email notifications automatically based on a rule. You plan to migrate the application to Azure.

You need to recommend a server-less computing solution for the application.
What should you include in the recommendation?

A. a web app
B. a server image in Azure Marketplace
C. a logic app
D. an API app

Correct Answer: C

Explanation/Reference:

Explanation:
Azure Logic Apps is a cloud service that helps you schedule, automate, and orchestrate tasks, business processes, and workflows when you need to integrate apps, data, systems, and services across enterprises or organizations. Logic Apps simplifies how you design and build scalable solutions for app integration, data integration, system integration, enterprise application integration (EAI), and business-to-business (B2B) communication, whether in the cloud, on premises, or both.

For example, here are just a few workloads you can automate with logic apps:
*   Process and route orders across on-premises systems and cloud services.
*   Send email notifications with Office 365 when events happen in various systems, apps, and services.
*   Move uploaded files from an SFTP or FTP server to Azure Storage.
*   Monitor tweets for a specific subject, analyze the sentiment, and create alerts or tasks for items that need review.

References:
https://docs.microsoft.com/en-us/azure/logic-apps/logic-apps-overview

QUESTION 35

You plan to deploy a website to Azure. The website will be accessed by users worldwide and will host large video files. You need to recommend which Azure feature must be used to provide the best video playback experience.

What should you recommend?

A. an application gateway
B. an Azure ExpressRoute circuit
C. a content delivery network (CDN)
D. an Azure Traffic Manager profile

Correct Answer: C

Explanation/Reference:

Explanation:
The question states that users are located worldwide and will be downloading large video files. The video playback experience would be improved if they can download the video from servers in the same region as the users. We can achieve this by using a content delivery network.

A content delivery network (CDN) is a distributed network of servers that can efficiently deliver web content to users. CDNs store cached content on edge servers in point-of-presence (POP) locations that are close to end users, to minimize latency.

Azure Content Delivery Network (CDN) offers developers a global solution for rapidly delivering high-bandwidth content to users by caching their content at strategically placed physical nodes across the world. Azure CDN can also accelerate dynamic content, which cannot be cached, by leveraging various network optimizations using CDN POPs. For example, route optimization to bypass Border Gateway Protocol (BGP).

The benefits of using Azure CDN to deliver web site assets include:
• Better performance and improved user experience for end users, especially when using applications in which multiple

round-trips are required to load content.
- Large scaling to better handle instantaneous high loads, such as the start of a product launch event.
- Distribution of user requests and serving of content directly from edge servers so that less traffic is sent to the origin server.

References:
https://docs.microsoft.com/en-us/azure/cdn/cdn-overview

QUESTION 36

Your company plans to deploy several million sensors that will upload data to Azure.

You need to identify which Azure resources must be created to support the planned solution. Which two Azure resources should you identify? Each correct answer presents part of the solution.

A. Azure Data Lake
B. Azure Queue storage
C. Azure File Storage
D. Azure IoT Hub
E. Azure Notification Hubs

Correct Answer: AD

Explanation/Reference:

Explanation:
IoT Hub (Internet of things Hub) provides data from millions of sensors.

IoT Hub is a managed service, hosted in the cloud, that acts as a central message hub for bi-directional communication between your IoT application and the devices it manages. You can use Azure IoT Hub to build IoT solutions with reliable and secure communications between millions of IoT devices and a cloud-hosted solution backend. You can connect virtually any device to IoT Hub.

There are two storage services IoT Hub can route messages to -- Azure Blob Storage and Azure Data Lake Storage Gen2 (ADLS Gen2) accounts. Azure Data Lake Storage accounts are hierarchical namespace-enabled storage accounts built on top of blob storage. Both of these use blobs for their storage.

References:
https://docs.microsoft.com/en-us/azure/iot-hub/about-iot-hub
https://docs.microsoft.com/en-us/azure/iot-hub/iot-hub-devguide-messages-d2c

QUESTION 37

Your company plans to deploy an Artificial Intelligence (AI) solution in Azure.

What should the company use to build, test, and deploy predictive analytics solutions?

A. Azure Logic Apps
B. Azure Machine Learning Studio
C. Azure Batch
D. Azure Cosmos DB

Correct Answer: B

Explanation/Reference:

Explanation:
Microsoft Azure Machine Learning Studio (classic) is a collaborative, drag-and-drop tool you can use to build, test, and deploy predictive analytics solutions on your data. Azure Machine Learning Studio (classic) publishes models as web services that can easily be consumed by custom apps or BI tools such as Excel.

Machine Learning Studio (classic) is where data science, predictive analytics, cloud resources, and your data meet.

References:
https://docs.microsoft.com/en-us/azure/machine-learning/studio/what-is-ml-studio

QUESTION 38

This question requires that you evaluate the underlined text to determine if it is correct.

Data that is stored in the Archive access tier of an Azure Storage account <u>can be accessed at any time by using azcopy.exe</u>.

A. No change is needed.
B. can only be read by using Azure Backup
C. must be restored before the data can be accessed
D. must be rehydrated before the data can be accessed

Correct Answer: D

Explanation/Reference:

Explanation:
Azure storage offers different access tiers: hot, cool and archive.

The archive access tier has the lowest storage cost. But it has higher data retrieval costs compared to the hot and cool tiers. Data in the archive tier can take several hours to retrieve.

While a blob is in archive storage, the blob data is offline and can't be read, overwritten, or modified. To read or download a blob in archive, you must first rehydrate it to an online tier.

Example usage scenarios for the archive access tier include:

Long-term backup, secondary backup, and archival datasets Original (raw) data that must be preserved, even after it has been processed into final usable form. Compliance and archival data that needs to be stored for a long time and is hardly ever accessed.

References:
https://docs.microsoft.com/en-us/azure/storage/blobs/storage-blob-storage-tiers?tabs=azure-portal#archive-access-tier

QUESTION 39

You have an Azure subscription named Subscription1. You sign in to the Azure portal and create a resource group named RG1. From Azure documentation, you have the following command that creates a virtual machine named VM1.

```
az vm create --resource-group RG1 --name VM1 --
image UbuntuLTS --generate-ssh-keys
```

You need to create VM1 in Subscription1 by using the command.

Solution: From the Azure portal, launch Azure Cloud Shell and select PowerShell. Run the command in Cloud Shell. Does this meet the goal?

A. Yes
B. No

Correct Answer: A

Explanation/Reference:

Explanation:
The command can be run in the Azure Cloud Shell. Although this question says you select PowerShell rather than Bash, the Az commands will work in PowerShell.

The Azure Cloud Shell is a free interactive shell. It has common Azure tools preinstalled and configured to use with your account.

To open the Cloud Shell, just select Try it from the upper right corner of a code block. You can also launch Cloud Shell in a separate browser tab by going to https:// shell.azure.com/bash.

Reference:
https://docs.microsoft.com/en-us/azure/virtual-machines/linux/quick-create-cli

QUESTION 40

Note: This question is part of a series of questions that present the same scenario. Each question in the series contains a unique solution that might meet the stated goals. Some question sets might have more than one correct solution, while others might not have a correct solution.

You have an Azure subscription named Subscription1. You sign in to the Azure portal and create a resource group named RG1.

From Azure documentation, you have the following command that creates a virtual machine named VM1.

```
az vm create --resource-group RG1 --name VM1 --
image UbuntuLTS --generate-ssh-keys
```

You need to create VM1 in Subscription1 by using the command.

Solution: From a computer that runs Windows 10, install Azure CLI. From PowerShell, sign in to Azure and then run the command. Does this meet the goal?

A. Yes
B. No

Correct Answer: A

Explanation/Reference:

Explanation:
The command can be run from PowerShell or the command prompt if you have the Azure CLI installed.

References:
https://docs.microsoft.com/en-us/cli/azure/install-azure-cli-windows?view=azure-cli-latest

QUESTION 41

Note: This question is part of a series of questions that present the same scenario. Each question in the series contains a unique solution that might meet the stated goals. Some question sets might have more than one correct solution, while others might not have a correct solution.

You have an Azure subscription named Subscription1. You sign in to the Azure portal and create a resource group named RG1. From Azure documentation, you have the following command that creates a virtual machine named VM1.

```
az vm create --resource-group RG1 --name VM1 --
image UbuntuLTS --generate-ssh-keys
```

You need to create VM1 in Subscription1 by using the command.

Solution: From a computer that runs Windows 10, install Azure CLI. From a command prompt, sign in to Azure and then run the command.

Does this meet the goal?

A. Yes
B. No

Correct Answer: A

Explanation/Reference:

Explanation:
The command can be run from PowerShell or the command prompt if you have the Azure CLI installed.

References:
https://docs.microsoft.com/en-us/cli/azure/install-azure-cli-windows?view=azure-cli-latest

QUESTION 42

This question requires that you evaluate the underlined text to determine if it is correct.

<u>Azure policies provide</u> a common platform for deploying objects to a cloud infrastructure and for implementing consistency across the Azure environment.

Instructions: Review the underlined text. If it makes the statement correct, select "No change is needed". If the statement is incorrect, select the answer choice that makes the statement correct.

A. No change is needed
B. Resource groups provide
C. Azure Resource Manager templates provides
D. Management groups provide

Correct Answer: C

Explanation/Reference:

Explanation:
<u>Azure Resource Manager templates provides</u> a common platform for deploying objects to a cloud infrastructure and for implementing consistency across the Azure environment.

Azure policies are used to define rules for what can be deployed and how it should be deployed. Whilst this can help in ensuring consistency, Azure policies do not provide the common platform for deploying objects to a cloud infrastructure.

References:
https://docs.microsoft.com/en-us/azure/governance/policy/overview

QUESTION 43

Note: This question is part of a series of questions that present the same scenario. Each question in the series contains a unique solution that might meet the stated goals. Some question sets might have more than one correct solution, while others might not have a correct solution.

An Azure administrator plans to run a PowerShell script that creates Azure resources. You need to recommend which computer configuration to use to run the script.

Solution: Run the script from a computer that runs Windows 10 and has the Azure PowerShell module installed. Does this meet the goal?

A. Yes
B. No

Correct Answer: A

Explanation/Reference:

Explanation:
A PowerShell script is a file that contains PowerShell cmdlets and code. A PowerShell script needs to be run in PowerShell. In this question, the computer has the Azure PowerShell module installed. Therefore, this solution does meet the goal.

References:
https://docs.microsoft.com/en-us/powershell/scripting/components/ise/how-to-write-and-run-scripts-in-the-windows-powershell-ise?view=powershell-6

QUESTION 44

Which service provides server-less computing in Azure?

A. Azure Virtual Machines
B. Azure Functions
C. Azure storage account
D. Azure Container Instances

Correct Answer: B

Explanation/Reference:

Explanation:
Azure Functions provide a platform for server-less code.
Azure Functions is a server-less compute service that lets you run event-triggered code without having to explicitly provision or manage infrastructure.

References:
https://docs.microsoft.com/en-us/azure/azure-functions/

QUESTION 45

You have an Azure subscription named Subscription1. You sign in to the Azure portal and create a resource group named RG1. From Azure documentation, you have the following command that creates a virtual machine named VM1.

```
az vm create --resource-group RG1 --name VM1 --
image UbuntuLTS --generate-ssh-keys
```

You need to create VM1 in Subscription1 by using the command.

Solution: From the Azure portal, launch Azure Cloud Shell and select **Bash**. Run the command in Cloud Shell. Does this meet the goal?

A. Yes
B. No

Correct Answer: A

Explanation/Reference:

Explanation:
The command can be run in the Azure Cloud Shell.

The Azure Cloud Shell is a free interactive shell. It has common Azure tools preinstalled and configured to use with your account.

To open the Cloud Shell, just select Try it from the upper right corner of a code block. You can also launch Cloud Shell in a separate browser tab by going to https:// shell.azure.com/bash.

References:
https://docs.microsoft.com/en-us/azure/virtual-machines/linux/quick-create-cli

QUESTION 46

Your company has several business units.

Each business unit requires 20 different Azure resources for daily operation. All the business units require the same type of Azure resources. You need to recommend a solution to automate the creation of the Azure resources.

What should you include in the recommendations?

A. Azure Resource Manager templates
B. virtual machine scale sets
C. the Azure API Management service
D. management groups

Correct Answer: A

Explanation/Reference:

Explanation:
You can use Azure Resource Manager templates to automate the creation of the Azure resources. Deploying resource through templates is known as 'Infrastructure as code'.

To implement infrastructure as code for your Azure solutions, use Azure Resource Manager templates. The template is a JavaScript Object Notation (JSON) file that defines the infrastructure and configuration for your project. The template uses declarative syntax, which lets you state what you intend to deploy without having to write the sequence of programming commands to create it. In the template, you specify the resources to deploy and the properties for those resources.

References:
https://docs.microsoft.com/en-us/azure/azure-resource-manager/templates/overview

QUESTION 47

Which Azure service should you use to correlate events from multiple resources into a centralized repository?

A. Azure Event Hubs
B. Azure Analysis Services
C. Azure Monitor
D. Azure Stream Analytics

Correct Answer: A

Explanation/Reference:

Explanation:
Azure Event Hubs is a big data streaming platform and event ingestion service. It can receive and process millions of events per second. Data sent to an event hub can be transformed and stored by using any real-time analytics provider or batching/storage adapters.

Azure Event Hubs can be used to ingest, buffer, store, and process your stream in real time to get actionable insights. Event Hubs uses a partitioned consumer model, enabling multiple applications to process the stream concurrently and letting you control the speed of processing.

Azure Event Hubs can be used to capture your data in near-real time in an Azure Blob storage or Azure Data Lake Storage for long-term retention or micro-batch processing.

References:
https://docs.microsoft.com/en-us/azure/event-hubs/event-hubs-about

QUESTION 48

Note: This question is part of a series of questions that present the same scenario. Each question in the series contains a unique solution that might meet the stated goals. Some question sets might have more than one correct solution, while others might not have a correct solution.

You have an Azure environment. You need to create a new Azure virtual machine from a tablet that runs the Android operating system. Solution: You use PowerShell in Azure Cloud Shell.

Does this meet the goal?

A. Yes
B. No

Correct Answer: A

Explanation/Reference:

Explanation:
Azure Cloud Shell is a browser-based shell experience to manage and develop Azure resources.

Cloud Shell offers a browser-accessible, pre-configured shell experience for managing Azure resources without the overhead of installing, versioning, and maintaining a machine yourself.

Being browser-based, Azure Cloud Shell can be run on a browser from a tablet that runs the Android operating system.

References:
https://docs.microsoft.com/en-us/azure/cloud-shell/features

QUESTION 49

This question requires that you evaluate the underlined text to determine if it is correct.

Azure Databricks is an Apache Spark-based analytics service.

Instructions: Review the underlined text. If it makes the statement correct, select "No change is needed." If the statement is incorrect, select the answer choice that makes the statement correct.

A. No change is needed.
B. Azure Data Factory
C. Azure DevOps
D. Azure HDInsight

Correct Answer: A

Explanation/Reference:

Explanation:
Azure Databricks is an Apache Spark-based analytics platform. The platform consists of several components including 'MLib'. Mlib is a Machine Learning library consisting of common learning algorithms and utilities, including classification, regression, clustering, collaborative filtering, dimensionality reduction, as well as underlying optimization primitives.

References:

https://docs.microsoft.com/en-us/azure/azure-databricks/what-is-azure-databricks#apache-spark-based-analytics-platform

QUESTION 50

You need to configure an Azure solution that meets the following requirements:

- Secures websites from attacks
- Generates reports that contain details of attempted attacks

What should you include in the solution?

A. Azure Firewall
B. a network security group (NSG)
C. Azure Information Protection
D. DDoS protection

Correct Answer: D

Explanation/Reference:

Explanation:
DDoS is a type of attack that tries to exhaust application resources. The goal is to affect the application's availability and its ability to handle legitimate requests. DDoS attacks can be targeted at any endpoint that is publicly reachable through the internet.

Azure has two DDoS service offerings that provide protection from network attacks: DDoS Protection Basic and DDoS Protection Standard. DDoS Basic protection is integrated into the Azure platform by default and at no extra cost.

You have the option of paying for DDoS Standard. It has several advantages over the basic service, including logging, alerting, and telemetry. DDoS Standard can generate reports that contain details of attempted attacks as required in this question.

References:
https://docs.microsoft.com/en-us/azure/security/fundamentals/ddos-best-practices

QUESTION 51

Your company plans to migrate all on-premises data to Azure. You need to identify whether Azure complies with the company's regional requirements. What should you use?

A. the Knowledge Center
B. Azure Marketplace
C. the Azure portal
D. the Trust Center

Correct Answer: D

Explanation/Reference:

Explanation:
Azure has more than 90 compliance certifications, including over 50 specific to global regions and countries, such as the US, the European Union, Germany, Japan, the United Kingdom, India and China.

You can view a list of compliance certifications in the Trust Center to determine whether Azure meets your regional requirements.

References:
https://azure.microsoft.com/en-gb/overview/trusted-cloud/compliance/ https://docs.microsoft.com/en-us/microsoft-365/compliance/get-started-with-service-trust-portal

QUESTION 52

This question requires that you evaluate the underlined text to determine if it is correct.

Azure Key Vault is used to store secrets for <u>Azure Active Directory (Azure AD) user accounts</u>.

Instructions: Review the underlined text. If it makes the statement correct, select "No change is needed". If the statement is incorrect, select the answer choice that makes the statement correct.

A. No change is needed
B. Azure Active Directory (Azure AD) administrative accounts
C. Personally Identifiable Information (PII)
D. server applications

Correct Answer: D

Explanation/Reference:

Explanation:
Centralizing storage of application secrets in Azure Key Vault allows you to control their distribution. Key Vault greatly reduces the chances that secrets may be accidentally leaked. When using Key Vault, application developers no longer need to store security information in their application. Not having to store security information in applications eliminates the need to make this information part of the code. For example, an application may need to connect to a database. Instead of storing the connection string in the app's code, you can store it securely in Key Vault.

References:
https://docs.microsoft.com/en-us/azure/key-vault/key-vault-overview https://docs.microsoft.com/en-us/learn/modules/manage-secrets-with-azure-key-vault/

QUESTION 53

You plan to deploy several Azure virtual machines.

You need to control the ports that devices on the Internet can use to access the virtual machines. What should you use?

A. a network security group (NSG)
B. an Azure Active Directory (Azure AD) role
C. an Azure Active Directory group
D. an Azure key vault

Correct Answer: A

Explanation/Reference:

Explanation:
A network security group works like a firewall. You can attach a network security group to a virtual network and/or individual subnets within the virtual network. You can also attach a network security group to a network interface assigned to a virtual machine. You can use multiple network security groups within a virtual network to restrict traffic between resources such as virtual machines and subnets.

You can filter network traffic to and from Azure resources in an Azure virtual network with a network security group. A network security group contains security rules that allow or deny inbound network traffic to, or outbound network traffic from, several types of Azure resources.

References:
https://docs.microsoft.com/en-us/azure/virtual-network/security-overview

QUESTION 54

This question requires that you evaluate the underlined text to determine if it is correct.

If a resource group named RG1 has a delete lock, <u>only a member of the global administrators group</u> can delete RG1.

Instructions: Review the underlined text. If it makes the statement correct, select "No change is needed". If the statement is incorrect, select the answer choice that makes the statement correct.

A. No change is needed
B. the delete lock must be removed before an administrator
C. an Azure policy must be modified before an administrator
D. an Azure tag must be added before an administrator

Correct Answer: B

Explanation/Reference:
Explanation:
You can configure a lock on a resource group to prevent the accidental deletion of the resource group. The lock applies to everyone, including global administrators. If you want to delete the resource group, the lock must be removed first.

As an administrator, you may need to lock a subscription, resource group, or resource to prevent other users in your organization from accidentally deleting or modifying critical resources. You can set the lock level to **CanNotDelete** or **ReadOnly**. In the portal, the locks are called **Delete** and **Read-only** respectively.

- **CanNotDelete** means authorized users can still read and modify a resource, but they can't delete the resource.
- **ReadOnly** means authorized users can read a resource, but they can't delete or update the resource. Applying this lock is similar to restricting all authorized users to the permissions granted by the **Reader** role.

Reference:
https://docs.microsoft.com/en-us/azure/azure-resource-manager/resource-group-lock-resources

QUESTION 55

This question requires that you evaluate the underlined text to determine if it is correct.

After you create a virtual machine, you need to modify the network security group (NSG) to allow connections to TCP port 8080 on the virtual machine.

Instructions: Review the underlined text. If it makes the statement correct, select "No change is needed". If the statement is incorrect, select the answer choice that makes the statement correct.

A. No change is needed
B. virtual network gateway
C. virtual network
D. route table

Correct Answer: A

Explanation/Reference:

Explanation:
When you create a virtual machine, the default setting is to create a Network Security Group attached to the network interface assigned to a virtual machine.

A network security group works like a firewall. You can attach a network security group to a virtual network and/or individual subnets within the virtual network. You can also attach a network security group to a network interface assigned to a virtual machine. You can use multiple network security groups within a virtual network to restrict traffic between resources such as virtual machines and subnets.

You can filter network traffic to and from Azure resources in an Azure virtual network with a network security group. A network security group contains security rules that allow or deny inbound network traffic to, or outbound network traffic from, several types of Azure resources.

In this question, we need to add a rule to the network security group to allow the connection to the virtual machine on port 8080.

References:
https://docs.microsoft.com/en-us/azure/virtual-network/security-overview

QUESTION 56

Your Azure environment contains multiple Azure virtual machines.

You need to ensure that a virtual machine named VM1 is accessible from the Internet over HTTP. Solution: You modify a network security group (NSG).

Does this meet the goal?

A. Yes
B. No

Correct Answer: A

Explanation/Reference:

Explanation:
A network security group works like a firewall. You can attach a network security group to a virtual network and/or individual subnets within the virtual network. You can also attach a network security group to a network interface assigned to a virtual machine. You can use multiple network security groups within a virtual network to restrict traffic between resources such as virtual machines and subnets.

You can filter network traffic to and from Azure resources in an Azure virtual network with a network security group. A network security group contains security rules that allow or deny inbound network traffic to, or outbound network traffic from, several types of Azure resources.

In this question, we need to add a rule to the network security group to allow the connection to the virtual machine on port 80 (HTTP).

References:
https://docs.microsoft.com/en-us/azure/virtual-network/security-overview

QUESTION 57

Note: This question is part of a series of questions that present the same scenario. Each question in the series contains a unique solution that might meet the stated goals. Some question sets might have more than one correct solution, while others might not have a correct solution.

Your Azure environment contains multiple Azure virtual machines.

You need to ensure that a virtual machine named VM1 is accessible from the Internet over HTTP. Solution: You modify a DDoS protection plan.

Does this meet the goal?

A. Yes
B. No

Correct Answer: B

Explanation/Reference:

Explanation:
DDoS is a form of attack on a network resource. A DDoS protection plan is used to protect against DDoS attacks; it does not provide connectivity to a virtual machine.

To ensure that a virtual machine named VM1 is accessible from the Internet over HTTP, you need to modify a network security group or Azure Firewall.

References:
https://docs.microsoft.com/en-us/azure/virtual-network/ddos-protection-overview

QUESTION 58

Note: This question is part of a series of questions that present the same scenario. Each question in the series contains a unique solution that might meet the stated goals. Some question sets might have more than one correct solution, while others might not have a correct solution.

Your Azure environment contains multiple Azure virtual machines.

You need to ensure that a virtual machine named VM1 is accessible from the Internet over HTTP. Solution: You modify an Azure firewall.

Does this meet the goal?

A. Yes
B. No

Correct Answer: A

Explanation/Reference:

Explanation:
Azure Firewall is a managed, cloud-based network security service that protects your Azure Virtual Network resources. It's a fully stateful firewall as a service with built-in high availability and unrestricted cloud scalability.

In this question, we need to add a rule to Azure Firewall to allow the connection to the virtual machine on port 80 (HTTP).

References:
https://docs.microsoft.com/en-us/azure/firewall/overview

QUESTION 59

Note: This question is part of a series of questions that present the same scenario. Each question in the series contains a unique solution that might meet the stated goals. Some question sets might have more than one correct solution, while others might not have a correct solution.

Your Azure environment contains multiple Azure virtual machines.

You need to ensure that a virtual machine named VM1 is accessible from the Internet over HTTP. Solution: You modify an Azure Traffic Manager profile.

Does this meet the goal?

A. Yes
B. No

Correct Answer: B

Explanation/Reference:

Explanation:
Azure Traffic Manager is a DNS-based load balancing solution. It is not used to ensure that a virtual machine named VM1 is accessible from the Internet over HTTP.

To ensure that a virtual machine named VM1 is accessible from the Internet over HTTP, you need to modify a network security group or Azure Firewall. In this question, we need to add a rule to a network security group or Azure Firewall to allow the connection to the virtual machine on port 80 (HTTP).

References:
https://docs.microsoft.com/en-us/azure/traffic-manager/traffic-manager-overview

QUESTION 60

Which two types of customers are eligible to use Azure Government to develop a cloud solution? Each correct answer presents a complete solution.

A. a Canadian government contractor
B. a European government contractor
C. a United States government entity
D. a United States government contractor
E. a European government entity

Correct Answer: CD

Explanation/Reference:

Explanation:
Azure Government is a cloud environment specifically built to meet compliance and security requirements for US government. This mission-critical cloud delivers breakthrough innovation to U.S. government customers and their partners. Azure Government applies to government at any level — from state and local governments to federal agencies including Department of Defense agencies.

The key difference between Microsoft Azure and Microsoft Azure Government is that Azure Government is a sovereign cloud. It's a physically separated instance of Azure, dedicated to U.S. government workloads only. It's built exclusively for government agencies and their solution providers.

References:
https://docs.microsoft.com/en-us/learn/modules/intro-to-azure-government/2-what-is-azure-government

QUESTION 61

You need to ensure that when Azure Active Directory (Azure AD) users connect to Azure AD from the Internet by using an anonymous IP address, the users are prompted automatically to change their password.

Which Azure service should you use?

A. Azure AD Connect Health
B. Azure AD Privileged Identity Management
C. Azure Advanced Threat Protection (ATP)
D. Azure AD Identity Protection

Correct Answer: D

Explanation/Reference:

Explanation:
Azure AD Identity Protection includes two risk policies: sign-in risk policy and user risk policy. A sign-in risk represents the probability that a given authentication request isn't authorized by the identity owner.

There are several types of risk detection. One of them is Anonymous IP Address. This risk detection type indicates sign-ins from an anonymous IP address (for example, Tor browser or anonymous VPN). These IP addresses are typically used by actors who want to hide their login telemetry (IP address, location, device, etc.) for potentially malicious intent.

You can configure the sign-in risk policy to require that users change their password.

References:
https://docs.microsoft.com/en-us/azure/active-directory/identity-protection/howto-sign-in-risk-policy
https://docs.microsoft.com/en-us/azure/active-directory/identity-protection/concept-identity-protection-risks

QUESTION 62

Your company plans to deploy several web servers and several database servers to Azure.

You need to recommend an Azure solution to limit the types of connections from the web servers to the database servers.
What should you include in the recommendation?

A. network security groups (NSGs)
B. Azure Service Bus
C. a local network gateway
D. a route filter

Correct Answer: A

Explanation/Reference:

Explanation:
A network security group works like a firewall. You can attach a network security group to a virtual network and/or individual subnets within the virtual network. You can also attach a network security group to a network interface assigned to a virtual machine. You can use multiple network security groups within a virtual network to restrict traffic between resources such as virtual machines and subnets.

You can filter network traffic to and from Azure resources in an Azure virtual network with a network security group. A network security group contains security rules that allow or deny inbound network traffic to, or outbound network traffic from, several types of Azure resources.

References:
https://docs.microsoft.com/en-us/azure/virtual-network/security-overview

QUESTION 63

Resource groups provide organizations with the ability to manage the compliance of Azure resources across multiple subscriptions.

Instructions: Review the underlined text. If it makes the statement correct, select "No change is needed". If the statement is incorrect, select the answer choice that makes the statement correct.

A. No change is needed
B. Management groups
C. Azure policies
D. Azure App Service plans

Correct Answer: C

Explanation/Reference:

Explanation:
Azure policies can be used to define requirements for resource properties during deployment and for already existing resources. Azure Policy controls properties such as the types or locations of resources.

Azure Policy is a service in Azure that you use to create, assign, and manage policies. These policies enforce different rules and effects over your resources, so those resources stay compliant with your corporate standards and service level agreements. Azure Policy meets this need by evaluating your resources for non- compliance with assigned policies. All data stored by Azure Policy is encrypted at rest.

For example, you can have a policy to allow only a certain SKU size of virtual machines in your environment. Once this policy is implemented, new and existing resources are evaluated for compliance. With the right type of policy, existing resources can be brought into compliance.

References:
https://docs.microsoft.com/en-us/azure/governance/policy/overview

QUESTION 64

Your network contains an Active Directory forest. The forest contains 5,000 user accounts.

Your company plans to migrate all network resources to Azure and to decommission the on-premises data center. You need to recommend a solution to minimize the impact on users after the planned migration.

What should you recommend?

A. Implement Azure Multi-Factor Authentication (MFA)
B. Sync all the Active Directory user accounts to Azure Active Directory (Azure AD)
C. Instruct all users to change their password
D. Create a guest user account in Azure Active Directory (Azure AD) for each user

Correct Answer: B

Explanation/Reference:

Explanation:
To migrate to Azure and decommission the on-premises data center, you would need to create the 5,000 user accounts in Azure Active Directory. The easy way to do this is to sync all the Active Directory user accounts to Azure Active Directory (Azure AD). You can even sync their passwords to further minimize the impact on users.
The tool you would use to sync the accounts is Azure AD Connect. The Azure Active Directory Connect synchronization services (Azure AD Connect sync) is a main component of Azure AD Connect. It takes care of all the operations that are related to synchronize identity data between your on-premises environment and Azure AD.

References:
https://docs.microsoft.com/en-us/azure/active-directory/hybrid/how-to-connect-sync-whatis

QUESTION 65

This question requires that you evaluate the underlined text to determine if it is correct.

From Access Control (IAM), you can view which user turned off a specific virtual machine during the last 14 days.

Instructions: Review the underlined text. If it makes the statement correct, select "No change is needed". If the statement is incorrect, select the answer choice that makes the statement correct.

A. No change is needed
B. Azure Event Hubs
C. Azure Activity Log
D. Azure Service Health

Correct Answer: C

Explanation/Reference:

Explanation:
You would use the Azure Activity Log, not Access Control to view which user turned off a specific virtual machine during the last 14 days. Activity logs are kept for 90 days. You can query for any range of dates, as long as the starting date isn't more than 90 days in the past. In this question, we would create a filter to display shutdown operations on the virtual machine in the last 14 days.

References:
https://docs.microsoft.com/en-us/azure/azure-resource-manager/resource-group-audit

QUESTION 66

Which service provides network traffic filtering across multiple Azure subscriptions and virtual networks?

A. Azure Firewall
B. an application security group
C. Azure DDoS protection
D. a network security group (NSG)

Correct Answer: A

Explanation/Reference:

Explanation:
You can restrict traffic to multiple virtual networks in multiple subscriptions with a single Azure firewall.

Azure Firewall is a managed, cloud-based network security service that protects your Azure Virtual Network resources. It's a fully stateful firewall as a service with built-in high availability and unrestricted cloud scalability.
You can centrally create, enforce, and log application and network connectivity policies across subscriptions and virtual networks. Azure Firewall uses a static public IP address for your virtual network resources allowing outside firewalls to identify traffic originating from your virtual network.

References:
https://docs.microsoft.com/en-us/azure/firewall/overview

QUESTION 67

Which Azure service should you use to store certificates?

A. Azure Security Center
B. an Azure Storage account
C. Azure Key Vault
D. Azure Information Protection

Correct Answer: C

Explanation/Reference:

Explanation:
Azure Key Vault is a secure store for storage various types of sensitive information including passwords and certificates.

Azure Key Vault can be used to securely store and tightly control access to tokens, passwords, certificates, API keys, and other secrets.
Secrets and keys are safeguarded by Azure, using industry-standard algorithms, key lengths, and hardware security modules (HSMs). The HSMs used are Federal Information Processing Standards (FIPS) 140-2 Level 2 validated.

Access to a key vault requires proper authentication and authorization before a caller (user or application) can get access. Authentication establishes the identity of the caller, while authorization determines the operations that they are allowed to perform.

References:
https://docs.microsoft.com/en-us/azure/key-vault/key-vault-overview

QUESTION 68

You have a resource group named RG1.

You plan to create virtual networks and app services in RG1.
You need to prevent the creation of virtual machines only in
RG1. What should you use?

A. a lock
B. an Azure role
C. a tag
D. an Azure policy

Correct Answer: D

Explanation/Reference:

Explanation:
Azure policies can be used to define requirements for resource
properties during deployment and for already existing
resources. Azure Policy controls properties such as the types or
locations of resources.

Azure Policy is a service in Azure that you use to create,
assign, and manage policies. These policies enforce different
rules and effects over your resources, so those resources stay
compliant with your corporate standards and service level
agreements.

In this question, we would create a Azure policy assigned to the
resource group that denies the creation of virtual machines in
the resource group.

You could place a read-only lock on the resource group.
However, that would prevent the creation of any resources in
the resource group, not virtual machines only. Therefore, an
Azure Policy is a better solution.

References:
https://docs.microsoft.com/en-
us/azure/governance/policy/overview

QUESTION 69

What can Azure Information Protection encrypt?

A. network traffic
B. documents and email messages
C. an Azure Storage account
D. an Azure SQL database

Correct Answer: B

Explanation/Reference:

Explanation:
Azure Information Protection can encrypt documents and emails.
Azure Information Protection is a cloud-based solution that helps an organization to classify and optionally, protect its documents and emails by applying labels. Labels can be applied automatically by administrators who define rules and conditions, manually by users, or a combination where users are given recommendations.

The protection technology uses Azure Rights Management (often abbreviated to Azure RMS). This technology is integrated with other Microsoft cloud services and applications, such as Office 365 and Azure Active Directory.

This protection technology uses encryption, identity, and authorization policies. Similarly to the labels that are applied, protection that is applied by using Rights Management stays with the documents and emails, independently of the location—inside or outside your organization, networks, file servers, and applications.

References:
https://docs.microsoft.com/en-us/azure/information-protection/what-is-information-protection
https://docs.microsoft.com/en-us/azure/information-protection/quickstart-label-dnf-protectedemail

QUESTION 70

What should you use to evaluate whether your company's Azure environment meets regulatory requirements?

A. the Knowledge Center website
B. the Advisor blade from the Azure portal
C. Compliance Manager from the Security Trust Portal
D. the Security Center blade from the Azure portal

Correct Answer: D

Explanation/Reference:

Explanation:
The Security Center blade from the Azure portal includes the 'regulatory compliance dashboard'.

The regulatory compliance dashboard provides insight into your compliance posture for a set of supported standards and regulations, based on continuous assessments of your Azure environment.
In the Azure Security Center regulatory compliance blade, you can get an overview of key portions of your compliance posture with respect to a set of supported standards. Currently supported standards are Azure CIS, PCI DSS 3.2, ISO 27001, and SOC TSP.

In the dashboard, you will find your overall compliance score, and the number of passing versus failing assessments with each standard. You can now focus your attention on the gaps in compliance for a standard or regulation that is important to you.

References:
https://azure.microsoft.com/en-us/blog/regulatory-compliance-dashboard-in-azure-security-center-now-available/

QUESTION 71

Your company implements <u>Azure policies</u> to automatically add a watermark to Microsoft Word documents that contain credit card information.

Instructions: Review the underlined text. If it makes the statement correct, select "No change is needed". If the statement is incorrect, select the answer choice that makes the statement correct.

A. No change is needed.
B. DDoS protection
C. Azure Information Protection
D. Azure Active Directory (Azure AD) Identity Protection

Correct Answer: C

Explanation/Reference:

Explanation:
Azure Information Protection is used to automatically add a watermark to Microsoft Word documents that contain credit card information.

You use Azure Information Protection labels to apply classification to documents and emails. When you do this, the classification is identifiable regardless of where the data is stored or with whom it's shared. The labels can include visual markings such as a header, footer, or watermark.

Labels can be applied automatically by administrators who define rules and conditions, manually by users, or a combination where users are given recommendations. In this question, we would configure a label to be automatically applied to Microsoft Word documents that contain credit card information. The label would then add the watermark to the documents.

References:
https://docs.microsoft.com/en-us/azure/information-protection/what-is-information-protection
https://docs.microsoft.com/en-us/azure/information-protection/infoprotect-quick-start-tutorial

QUESTION 72

This question requires that you evaluate the underlined text to determine if it is correct.

From <u>Azure Monitor</u>, you can view which user turned off a specific virtual machine during the last 14 days.
Instructions: Review the underlined text. If it makes the statement correct, select "No change is needed". If the statement is incorrect, select the answer choice that makes the statement correct.

A. No change is needed
B. Azure Event Hubs
C. Azure Activity Log
D. Azure Service Health

Correct Answer: C

Explanation/Reference:

Explanation:
You would use the Azure Activity Log, not Azure Monitor to view which user turned off a specific virtual machine during the last 14 days. Activity logs are kept for 90 days. You can query for any range of dates, as long as the starting date isn't more than 90 days in the past. In this question, we would create a filter to display shutdown operations on the virtual machine in the last 14 days.

References:
https://docs.microsoft.com/en-us/azure/azure-resource-manager/resource-group-audit

QUESTION 73

You have an Azure virtual network named VNET1 in a resource group named RG1.

You assign an Azure policy specifying that virtual networks are not an allowed resource type in RG1. VNET1 is deleted automatically.

Instructions: Review the underlined text. If it makes the statement correct, select "No change is needed". If the statement is incorrect, select the answer choice that makes the statement correct.

A. No change is needed
B. is moved automatically to another resource group
C. continues to function normally
D. is now a read-only object

Correct Answer: C

Explanation/Reference:

Explanation:
The VNet will be marked as 'Non-compliant' when the policy is assigned. However, it will not be deleted and will continue to function normally.
Azure Policy is a service in Azure that you use to create, assign, and manage policies. These policies enforce different rules and effects over your resources, so those resources stay compliant with your corporate standards and service level agreements.
If there are any existing resources that aren't compliant with a new policy assignment, they appear under **Non-compliant resources.**

References:
https://docs.microsoft.com/en-us/azure/governance/policy/overview
https://docs.microsoft.com/en-us/azure/governance/policy/assign-policy-portal

QUESTION 74

Your company has an Azure environment that contains resources in several regions.

A company policy states that administrators must only be allowed to create additional Azure resources in a region in the country where their office is located. You need to create the Azure resource that must be used to meet the policy requirement.

What should you create?

A. a read-only lock
B. an Azure policy
C. a management group
D. a reservation

Correct Answer: B

Explanation/Reference:

Explanation:
Azure policies can be used to define requirements for resource properties during deployment and for already existing resources. Azure Policy controls properties such as the types or locations of resources.

Azure Policy is a service in Azure that you use to create, assign, and manage policies. These policies enforce different rules and effects over your resources, so those resources stay compliant with your corporate standards and service level agreements. Azure Policy meets this need by evaluating your resources for non- compliance with assigned policies. All data stored by Azure Policy is encrypted at rest.

Azure Policy offers several built-in policies that are available by default. In this question, we would use the 'Allowed Locations' policy to define the locations where resources can be deployed.

References:
https://docs.microsoft.com/en-us/azure/governance/policy/overview

QUESTION 75

This question requires that you evaluate the underlined text to determine if it is correct.

From Azure Cloud Shell, you can track your company's regulatory standards and regulations, such as ISO 27001.

Instructions: Review the underlined text. If it makes the statement correct, select "No change is needed." If the statement is incorrect, select the answer choice that makes the statement correct.

A. No change is needed.
B. the Microsoft Cloud Partner Portal
C. Compliance Manager
D. the Trust Center

Correct Answer: C

Explanation/Reference:

Explanation:
Microsoft Compliance Manager (Preview) is a free workflow-based risk assessment tool that lets you track, assign, and verify regulatory compliance activities related to Microsoft cloud services. Azure Cloud Shell, on the other hand, is an interactive, authenticated, browser-accessible shell for managing Azure resources.

References:
https://docs.microsoft.com/en-us/microsoft-365/compliance/compliance-manager-overview
https://docs.microsoft.com/en-us/azure/cloud-shell/overview

QUESTION 76

This question requires that you evaluate the underlined text to determine if it is correct.

The <u>Microsoft Online Services Privacy Statement</u> explains what data Microsoft processes, how Microsoft processes the data, and the purpose of processing the data.

Instructions: Review the underlined text. If it makes the statement correct, select "No change is needed." If the statement is incorrect, select the answer choice that makes the statement correct.

A. No change is needed.
B. Microsoft Online Services Terms
C. Microsoft Online Service Level Agreement
D. Online Subscription Agreement for Microsoft Azure

Correct Answer: A

Explanation/Reference:

Explanation:
The Microsoft Privacy Statement explains what personal data Microsoft processes, how Microsoft processes the data, and the purpose of processing the data

References:
https://privacy.microsoft.com/en-us/privacystatement

QUESTION 77

This question requires that you evaluate the underlined text to determine if it is correct.

You have several virtual machines in an Azure subscription. You create a new subscription. <u>The virtual machines cannot be moved to the new subscription</u>.

Instructions: Review the underlined text. If it makes the statement correct, select "No change is needed". If the statement is incorrect, select the answer choice that makes the statement correct.

A. No change is needed
B. The virtual machines can be moved to the new subscription
C. The virtual machines can be moved to the new subscription only if they are all in the same resource group
D. The virtual machines can be moved to the new subscription only if they run Windows Server 2016.

Correct Answer: B

Explanation/Reference:

Explanation:
You can move a VM and its associated resources to a different subscription by using the Azure portal.
Moving between subscriptions can be handy if you originally created a VM in a personal subscription and now want to move it to your company's subscription to continue your work. You do not need to start the VM in order to move it and it should continue to run during the move.

References:
https://docs.microsoft.com/en-us/azure/virtual-machines/windows/move-vm

QUESTION 78

You attempt to create several managed Microsoft SQL Server instances in an Azure environment and receive a message that you must increase your Azure subscription limits.

What should you do to increase the limits?

A. Create a service health alert
B. Upgrade your support plan
C. Modify an Azure policy
D. Create a new support request

Correct Answer: D

Explanation/Reference:

Explanation:
Many Azure resource have quote limits. The purpose of the quota limits is to help you control your Azure costs. However, it is common to require an increase to the default quota.

You can request a quota limit increase by opening a support request. In the support request, select 'Service and subscription limits (quotas)' for the Issue type, select your subscription and the service you want to increase the quota for. For this question, you would select 'SQL Database Managed Instance' as the quote type.

References:
https://docs.microsoft.com/en-us/azure/sql-database/sql-database-managed-instance-resource-limits#obtaining-a-larger-quota-for-sql-managed-instance

QUESTION 79

Your company has 10 offices. You plan to generate several billing reports from the Azure portal. Each report will contain the Azure resource utilization of each office.

Which Azure Resource Manager feature should you use before you generate the reports?

A. tags
B. templates
C. locks
D. policies

Correct Answer: A

Explanation/Reference:

Explanation:
You can use resource tags to 'label' Azure resources. Tags are metadata elements attached to resources. Tags consist of pairs of key/value strings. In this question, we would tag each resource with a tag to identify each office. For example: Location = Office1. When all Azure resources are tagged, you can generate reports to list all resources based on the value of the tag. For example: All resources used by Office1.

References:
https://docs.microsoft.com/en-us/azure/cloud-adoption-framework/decision-guides/resource-tagging/

QUESTION 80

You deploy an Azure resource. The resource becomes unavailable for an extended period due to a service outage. Microsoft will <u>automatically refund your bank account</u>.

Instructions: Review the underlined text. If it makes the statement correct, select "No change is needed". If the statement is incorrect, select the answer choice that makes the statement correct.

A. No change is needed.
B. automatically migrate the resource to another subscription
C. automatically credit your account
D. send you a coupon code that you can redeem for Azure credits

Correct Answer: C

Explanation/Reference:

Explanation:
If the SLA for an Azure service is not met, you receive credits for that service and that service only. The credits are deducted from your monthly bill for that service. If you stopped using the service where the SLA was not met, your account would remain in credit for that service. The credits would not be applied to any other services that you may be using.

Service Credits apply only to fees paid for the particular Service, Service Resource, or Service tier for which a Service Level has not been met. In cases where Service Levels apply to individual Service Resources or to separate Service tiers, Service Credits apply only to fees paid for the affected Service Resource or Service tier, as applicable. The Service Credits awarded in any billing month for a particular Service or Service Resource will not, under any circumstance, exceed your monthly service fees for that Service or Service Resource, as applicable, in the billing month.

References:
https://azure.microsoft.com/en-gb/support/legal/sla/analysis-services/v1_0/

QUESTION 81

Your company plans to migrate to Azure. The company has several departments. All the Azure resources used by each department will be managed by a department administrator.

What are two possible techniques to segment Azure for the departments? Each correct answer presents a complete solution.

A. multiple subscriptions
B. multiple Azure Active Directory (Azure AD) directories
C. multiple regions
D. multiple resource groups

Correct Answer: AD

Explanation/Reference:

Explanation:
An Azure subscription is a container for Azure resources. It is also a boundary for permissions to resources and for billing. You are charged monthly for all resources in a subscription. A single Azure tenant (Azure Active Directory) can contain multiple Azure subscriptions.

A resource group is a container that holds related resources for an Azure solution. The resource group can include all the resources for the solution, or only those resources that you want to manage as a group.

To enable each department administrator to manage the Azure resources used by that department, you will need to create a separate subscription per department. You can then assign each department administrator as an administrator for the subscription to enable them to manage all resources in that subscription.

References:
https://docs.microsoft.com/en-us/azure/cost-management-billing/manage/create-subscription
https://docs.microsoft.com/en-us/azure/cost-management-billing/manage/add-change-subscription-administrator

QUESTION 82

This question requires that you evaluate the underlined text to determine if it is correct.

If Microsoft plans to end support for an Azure service that does NOT have a successor service, Microsoft will provide notification at least <u>12 months</u> before.

Instructions: Review the underlined text. If it makes the statement correct, select "No change is needed". If the statement is incorrect, select the answer choice that makes the statement correct.

A. No change is needed.
B. 6 months
C. 90 days
D. 30 days

Correct Answer: A

Explanation/Reference:

Explanation:
The Modern Lifecycle Policy covers products and services that are serviced and supported continuously. For products governed by the Modern Lifecycle Policy,

Microsoft will provide a minimum of 12 months' notification prior to ending support if no successor product or service is offered—excluding free services or preview releases.

Reference:
https://support.microsoft.com/en-us/help/30881

QUESTION 83

Note: This question is part of a series of questions that present the same scenario. Each question in the series contains a unique solution that might meet the stated goals. Some question sets might have more than one correct solution, while others might not have a correct solution.

Your company has an Azure subscription that contains the following unused resources:

- 20 user accounts in Azure Active Directory (Azure AD)
- Five groups in Azure AD
- 10 public IP addresses
- 10 network interfaces

You need to reduce the Azure costs for the company. Solution: You remove the unused network interfaces. Does this meet the goal?

A. Yes
B. No

Correct Answer: B

Explanation/Reference:

Explanation:
You are not charged for unused network interfaces. Therefore, deleting unused network interfaces will not reduce the Azure costs for the company.

References:
https://docs.microsoft.com/en-us/azure/advisor/advisor-cost-recommendations#reduce-costs-by-deleting-or-reconfiguring-idle-virtual-network-gateways

QUESTION 84

Note: This question is part of a series of questions that present the same scenario. Each question in the series contains a unique solution that might meet the stated goals. Some question sets might have more than one correct solution, while others might not have a correct solution.

Your company has an Azure subscription that contains the following unused resources:

- 20 user accounts in Azure Active Directory (Azure AD)
- Five groups in Azure AD
- 10 public IP addresses
- 10 network interfaces

You need to reduce the Azure costs for the company. Solution: You remove the unused public IP addresses. Does this meet the goal?

A. Yes
B. No

Correct Answer: A

Explanation/Reference:

Explanation:
You are charged for public IP addresses. Therefore, deleting unused public IP addresses will reduce the Azure costs.

References:
https://docs.microsoft.com/en-us/azure/advisor/advisor-cost-recommendations#reduce-costs-by-deleting-or-reconfiguring-idle-virtual-network-gateways

QUESTION 85

Note: This question is part of a series of questions that present the same scenario. Each question in the series contains a unique solution that might meet the stated goals. Some question sets might have more than one correct solution, while others might not have a correct solution.

Your company has an Azure subscription that contains the following unused resources:
- 20 user accounts in Azure Active Directory (Azure AD)
- Five groups in Azure AD
- 10 public IP addresses
- 10 network interfaces

You need to reduce the Azure costs for the company. Solution: You remove the unused user accounts.
Does this meet the goal?

A. Yes
B. No

Correct Answer: B

Explanation/Reference:

Explanation:
You are not charged for user accounts. Therefore, deleting unused user accounts will not reduce the Azure costs for the company.

References:
https://docs.microsoft.com/en-us/azure/advisor/advisor-cost-recommendations#reduce-costs-by-deleting-or-reconfiguring-idle-virtual-network-gateways

QUESTION 86

This question requires that you evaluate the underlined text to determine if it is correct.

A support plan solution that gives you best practice information, health status and notifications, and 24/7 access to billing information at the lowest possible cost is a <u>Standard</u> support plan.

Instructions: Review the underlined text. If it makes the statement correct, select "No change is needed". If the statement is incorrect, select the answer choice that makes the statement correct.

A. No change is needed
B. Developer
C. Basic
D. Premier

Correct Answer: C

Explanation/Reference:

Explanation:
A basic support plan provides:
- 24x7 access to billing and subscription support, online self-help, documentation, whitepapers, and support forums
- Best practices: Access to full set of Azure Advisor recommendations
- Health Status and Notifications: Access to personalized Service Health Dashboard & Health API

References:
https://azure.microsoft.com/en-us/support/plans/

QUESTION 87

In which Azure support plans can you open a new support request?

A. Premier and Professional Direct only
B. Premier, Professional Direct, and Standard only
C. Premier, Professional Direct, Standard, and Developer only
D. Premier, Professional Direct, Standard, Developer, and Basic

Correct Answer: C

Explanation/Reference:

Explanation:
You can open support cases in the following plans: Premier, Professional Direct, Standard, and Developer only. You cannot open support cases in the Basic support plan.

References:
https://azure.microsoft.com/en-us/support/plans/

QUESTION 88

This question requires that you evaluate the underlined text to determine if it is correct.

You can create an Azure support request from support.microsoft.com.

Instructions: Review the underlined text. If it makes the statement correct, select "No change is needed." If the statement is incorrect, select the answer choice that makes the statement correct.

A. No change is needed.
B. the Azure portal
C. the Knowledge Center
D. the Security & Compliance admin center

Correct Answer: B

Explanation/Reference:

Explanation:
You can create an Azure support request from the Help and Support blade in the Azure portal or from the context menu of an Azure resource in the Support + Troubleshooting section.

References:
https://docs.microsoft.com/en-us/azure/azure-supportability/how-to-create-azure-support-request

QUESTION 89

Note: This question is part of a series of questions that present the same scenario. Each question in the series contains a unique solution that might meet the stated goals. Some question sets might have more than one correct solution, while others might not have a correct solution.

Your company has an Azure subscription that contains the following unused resources:

- 20 user accounts in Azure Active Directory (Azure AD)
- Five groups in Azure AD
- 10 public IP addresses
- 10 network interfaces

You need to reduce the Azure costs for the company. Solution: You remove the unused groups.

Does this meet the goal?

A. Yes
B. No

Correct Answer: B

Explanation/Reference:

Explanation:
You are not charged for Azure Active Directory Groups. Therefore, deleting unused groups will not reduce your Azure costs.

References:
https://docs.microsoft.com/en-us/azure/advisor/advisor-cost-recommendations#reduce-costs-by-deleting-or-reconfiguring-idle-virtual-network-gateways

QUESTION 90

This question requires that you evaluate the underlined text to determine if it is correct.

All Azure services that are in public preview are <u>provided without any documentation</u>.

Instructions: Review the underlined text. If it makes the statement correct, select "No change is needed". If the statement is incorrect, select the answer choice that makes the statement correct.

A. No change is needed
B. only configurable from Azure CLI
C. excluded from the Service Level Agreements
D. only configurable from the Azure portal

Correct Answer: C

Explanation/Reference:
Explanation:
Preview features are made available to you on the condition that you accept additional terms which supplement the regular Azure terms. The supplemental terms state:

"PREVIEWS ARE PROVIDED "AS-IS," "WITH ALL FAULTS," AND "AS AVAILABLE," AND ARE EXCLUDED FROM THE SERVICE LEVEL AGREEMENTS AND LIMITED WARRANTY."

References:
https://azure.microsoft.com/en-gb/support/legal/preview-supplemental-terms/

QUESTION 91

What is guaranteed in an Azure Service Level Agreement (SLA) for virtual machines?

A. uptime
B. feature availability
C. bandwidth
D. performance

Correct Answer: A

Explanation/Reference:

Explanation:
The SLA for virtual machines guarantees 'uptime'. The amount of uptime guaranteed depends on factors such as whether the VMs are in an availability set or availability zone if there is more than one VM, the distribution of the VMs if there is more than one or the disk type if it is a single VM.

The SLA for Virtual Machines states:

- For all Virtual Machines that have two or more instances deployed across two or more Availability Zones in the same Azure region, we guarantee you will have Virtual Machine Connectivity to at least one instance at least 99.99% of the time.
- For all Virtual Machines that have two or more instances deployed in the same Availability Set or in the same Dedicated Host Group, we guarantee you will have Virtual Machine Connectivity to at least one instance at least 99.95% of the time.
- For any Single Instance Virtual Machine using Premium SSD or Ultra Disk for all Operating System Disks and Data Disks, we guarantee you will have Virtual Machine Connectivity of at least 99.9%.

References:
https://azure.microsoft.com/en-us/support/legal/sla/summary/
https://azure.microsoft.com/en-us/support/legal/sla/virtual-machines/v1_9/

QUESTION 92

Note: This question is part of a series of questions that present the same scenario. Each question in the series contains a unique solution that might meet the stated goals. Some question sets might have more than one correct solution, while others might not have a correct solution.

Your company plans to purchase Azure.

The company's support policy states that the Azure environment must provide an option to access support engineers by phone or email. You need to recommend which support plan meets the support policy requirement.
Solution: Recommend a Basic support plan. Does this meet the goal?

A. Yes
B. No

Correct Answer: B

Explanation/Reference:

Explanation:
The Basic support plan does not have any technical support for engineers.

Access to Support Engineers via email or phone is available in the following support plans: Premier, Professional Direct and standard.

References:
https://azure.microsoft.com/en-gb/support/plans/

QUESTION 93

Note: This question is part of a series of questions that present the same scenario. Each question in the series contains a unique solution that might meet the stated goals. Some question sets might have more than one correct solution, while others might not have a correct solution.

Your company plans to purchase Azure.

The company's support policy states that the Azure environment must provide an option to access support engineers by phone or email. You need to recommend which support plan meets the support policy requirement.

Solution: Recommend a Standard support plan. Does this meet the goal?

A. Yes
B. No

Correct Answer: A

Explanation/Reference:

Explanation:
The Standard, Professional Direct, and Premier support plans have technical support for engineers via email and phone.

References:
https://azure.microsoft.com/en-gb/support/plans/

QUESTION 94

Your company plans to request an architectural review of an Azure environment from Microsoft. The company currently has a Basic support plan.

You need to recommend a new support plan for the company. The solution must minimize costs. Which support plan should you recommend?

A. Premier
B. Developer
C. Professional Direct
D. Standard

Correct Answer: A

Explanation/Reference:

Explanation:
The Premier support plan provides customer specific architectural support such as design reviews, performance tuning, configuration and implementation assistance delivered by Microsoft Azure technical specialists.

References:
https://azure.microsoft.com/en-gb/support/plans/

QUESTION 95

What is required to use Azure Cost Management?

A. a Dev/Test subscription
B. Software Assurance
C. an Enterprise Agreement (EA)
D. a pay-as-you-go subscription

Correct Answer: C

Explanation/Reference:

Explanation:
Azure customers with an Azure Enterprise Agreement (EA),
Microsoft Customer Agreement (MCA), or Microsoft Partner
Agreement (MPA) can use Azure Cost Management.

Cost management is the process of effectively planning and
controlling costs involved in your business. Cost management
tasks are normally performed by finance, management, and app
teams. Azure Cost Management + Billing helps organizations
plan with cost in mind. It also helps to analyze costs effectively
and take action to optimize cloud spending.

References:
https://docs.microsoft.com/en-gb/azure/cost-
management/overview-cost-mgt

QUESTION 96

This question requires that you evaluate the underlined text to determine if it is correct.

Your Azure trial account expired last week. You are now unable to create additional <u>Azure Active Directory (Azure AD) user accounts</u>.

Instructions: Review the underlined text. If it makes the statement correct, select "No change is needed". If the statement is incorrect, select the answer choice that makes the statement correct.

A. No change is needed
B. start an existing Azure virtual machine
C. access your data stored in Azure
D. access the Azure portal

Correct Answer: B

Explanation/Reference:

Explanation:
A stopped (deallocated) VM is offline and not mounted on an Azure host server. Starting a VM mounts the VM on a host server before the VM starts. As soon as the VM is mounted, it becomes chargeable. For this reason, you are unable to start a VM after a trial has expired.

Incorrect Answers:
A: You are not charged for Azure Active Directory user accounts so you can continue to create accounts. C: You can access data that is already stored in Azure.

D: You can access the Azure Portal. You can also reactivate and upgrade the expired subscription in the portal.

QUESTION 97

Your company has 10 departments. The company plans to implement an Azure environment. You need to ensure that each department can use a different payment option for the Azure services it consumes. What should you create for each department?

A. a reservation
B. a subscription
C. a resource group
D. a container instance

Correct Answer: B

Explanation/Reference:
Explanation:
There are different payment options in Azure including pay-as-you-go (PAYG), Enterprise Agreement (EA), and Microsoft Customer Agreement (MCA) accounts. Your Azure costs are 'per subscription'. You are charged monthly for all resources in a subscription. Therefore, to use different payment options per department, you will need to create a separate subscription per department. You can create multiple subscriptions in a single Azure Active Directory tenant.

Incorrect Answers:
A: A reservation is where you commit to a resource (for example a virtual machine) for one or three years. This gives you a discounted price on the resource for the reservation period. Reservations do not provide a way to use different payment options per department.
C: A resource group is a logical container for Azure resources. You can view the total cost of all the resources in a resource group. However, resource groups do not provide a way to use different payment options per department.
D: A container instance is an Azure resource used to run an application. Container instances do not provide a way to use different payment options per department.

References:
https://docs.microsoft.com/en-us/azure/cost-management-billing/manage/create-subscription

QUESTION 98

This question requires that you evaluate the underlined text to determine if it is correct.

You can use <u>Advisor recommendations</u> in Azure to send email alerts when the cost of the current billing period for an Azure subscription exceeds a specified limit.

Instructions: Review the underlined text. If it makes the statement correct, select "No change is needed." If the statement is incorrect, select the answer choice that makes the statement correct.

A. No change is needed.
B. Access control (IAM)
C. Budget alerts
D. Compliance

Correct Answer: C

Explanation/Reference:

Explanation:
Budget alerts notify you when spending, based on usage or cost, reaches or exceeds the amount defined in the alert condition of the budget. Cost Management budgets are created using the Azure portal or the Azure Consumption API.

References:
https://docs.microsoft.com/en-us/azure/cost-management-billing/costs/cost-mgt-alerts-monitor-usage-spending